WEEGIE WIT & WISDOM

WEEGIE WIT & WISDOM

IAN BLACK

BLACK & WHITE PUBLISHING

First published 2006
by Black & White Publishing Ltd
99 Giles Street, Edinburgh EH6 6BZ

ISBN 10:   1 84502 124 X
ISBN 13:   978 1 84502 124 5

British Library Cataloguing in Publication Data:
A catalogue record for this book is available
from the British Library.

Printed and bound by Nørhaven Paperback A/S

CONTENTS

DEDICATION

This book is dedicated to every Glaswegian
who ever made a fool of his or herself.
That would be all of us, then.

INTRODUCTION

One of Glasgow's many great men, Charles Rennie Mackintosh, coined the aphorism: "There is hope in honest error; none in the icy perfections of the mere stylist," and this is in Glasgow's DNA, an inbuilt and unshakable belief that making a fool of yourself is okay, as long as it gets a laugh, makes a buck, builds a better society, or whatever. Nobody but a real fool never made an error, and we do laugh louder and we do try harder. It is part of who we are and what made us the holy eejits we can be, God love us.

Weegies have long been known for the quickness of their wit and the sharpness of their tongues, but possibly less for their deep philosophical stances on various issues and more for the surreality of the insult or threat. What do you make of a man who says: "You, ya bastard! Ah'm gonny stick your heid so far up your arse that you'll think that nothing has happened"?

This book is an attempt to link and examine these threads of Glaswegian culture, and if you laugh your arse off and/or learn a thing or two, well where's the harm?

I discovered my own philosophy of life on a

number 63 bus heading for Partick from outside the Barras, copying it from a lad in his teens sitting beside me. I'd had a lousy day at my stall, I'd got soaked waiting for the bus and I was almost broke. The young guy was a Down's syndrome child, what in harsher days we used to call a mongol. He was bubbly and cheerful, shaking his tambourine in everyone's faces, singing and smiling, asking everyone for a penny, and raising a few smiles from the passengers.

The conductor came up collecting his fares and I paid mine, noting that he didn't ask the young lad for his fare. When the conductor had moved a step or two up the bus the boy turned to me and said: "If you kid on you're daft, you get a free hurl."

It is still working for me.

1
WHY GLASWEGIANS DRINK

Because we can.

It has been wisely said that religions change, but beer and wine remain. Here are some thoughts on booze and the Glasgow attitude to it:

Do not allow children to mix drinks. It is unseemly and they put in too much tonic.

Alcohol is good for you. My grandfather proved it irrevocably. He drank two bottles of booze every mature day of his life and lived to the age of 103. I was at the cremation. That fire would just not go out.

Drink affects Weegies in different ways. Some get nasty, some get funny. I have a friend called Laura who is a social worker, a counsellor of alcoholics in fact, but who likes the odd pint. We were standing chatting in a corner of the Doublet Bar when she pointed out a guy sitting at a table and said that she reckoned he was drinking to nerve himself up to something. She was right. Uninvited, he came over and rudely pushed himself between us, turned his back on me, and rather aggressively offered to buy Laura a drink. As he was doing so he produced a huge roll of tenners from his pocket. It was instantly apparent that only the outside one was real. I've read about people who do this but had never actually met one.

Laura politely declined his offer, but he persisted, waving his fake wad around and making disparaging remarks about my physique, as opposed to his, as he was a well-built bloke with huge biceps. After a minute or so of posturing and bluster he stood in front of Laura and flexed his biceps, asking: "What do you think of that, then?"

Laura coolly looked him up and down, stared him in the eye and said, in tones of polite enquiry: "You wank with both hands?"

There are difficult words for Weegies to say when drunk, like statistician, innovative, preliminary and proliferation, and there are words that you will never hear a Glaswegian say, no matter how drunk he or she is. Here are a couple:

No, I don't want another drink

No kebab/raw octupus/hedgehog burger for me, thanks

Sorry, but you are not quite good looking enough for me

Good evening, officer

*Thanks, but I don't want to get up on the stage
and sing karaoke*

No more for me thanks, I've had sufficient

No, I would not be interested in taking part

Be quiet!

These trousers are far too bright for me to wear

Please shut up everyone, I'm trying to watch the game

No thanks, I don't dance

I couldn't drink another drop

*I wish they'd just shut the bar so we can all
go home early*

Are you sure they don't clash?

13

Some new Weegie definitions

Reintartanation: Coming back as a footsoldier in the Tartan Army.

Balderdash: a rapidly receding hairline.

Semantics: Pranks conducted by young men studying for the priesthood, including such things as gluing the pages of the priest's prayer book together just before vespers.

Foreploy: Any misrepresentation about yourself for the purpose of obtaining sexual congress.

Giraffiti: Vandalism spray-painted very, very high.

Ignoranus: A person who's both stupid and an arsehole.

Cross-cut purposes

The Weegie on the second day of his holiday in the Highlands watched Calum and his son sawing a log with a cross-cut saw. Suddenly he called furiously to the far-mer: "Let the wee man have it, ya big bullying bastard!"

Weegie Jimmy had been greeted by the stunning news that he was to become a father for the first time. Jumping with joy, he couldn't wait to go out and celebrate with his pals, but first he must tend to the needs of his lovely wife Kate.

"Now darling, I'm just popping along the road for a few minutes. Is there anything you'd like while I'm out?"

"Yes," said Kate. "I'd like you to buy some snails. I just fancy cooking them in garlic butter tonight. So don't be long, will you?"

"I'll be back before you know it," promised Jimmy, full of good intentions.

Two hours later, bag of snails in hand, he was still propping up the bar and wetting the baby's head for the umpteenth time. Finally he decided to do the right thing, bade farewell to his mates and stumbled out into the night. Weaving from side to side, he eventually reached his house and tottered up towards the door. In trying to get his keys out of his pocket, he dropped the bag of snails and it split open on the step, scattering snails everywhere.

The noise woke Kate who opened the bedroom window and shouted down:

"What's going on? Where have you been all this time?"

Jimmy looked down at the snails, clapped his hands and said: "Come on, boys! We're nearly home!"

An early Glasgow man was condemned to receive forty lashes, but the more they whipped him the more he laughed.

"What's so funny?" they asked him.

"You don't understand," he told them, helpless with laughter. "You're whipping the wrong man".

"Da," asked the Glasgow five-year-old, "what makes children delinquent?"

"Shut up, son. Pour yourself another drink and deal."

An alcoholic has been defined as a man who drinks more than his doctor.

Be always drunken. Nothing else matters . . .
Drunken with what?

With wine, with poetry, or with virtue, as you will.
But be drunken.
I am singing the best song ever was sung
And it has a rousing chorus.

Baudelaire

Wine is the last companion.

Glaswegian reply when informed that the particular
drink he was drinking was slow poison:
"So who's in a hurry?"

These two Glaswegians were passing a pub. Well, it
could happen.

A teetotaller has been defined as, "A weak person
who yields to the temptation of denying himself a
pleasure."

The trouble with the world is that everyone is a few
drinks behind.

Judge: Were you drunk at 4am?
Weegie: Isn't everybody?

Sage advice: Never accept a drink from a urologist.

The hard part about being a bartender is figuring out who is drunk and who is just stupid.

Beer that is not drunk has missed its vocation.

How come, if alcohol kills millions of brain cells, it never killed the ones that made me want to drink?

Never cry over spilt milk. It could have been whisky.

A meal without wine is like a day without sunshine.

Senga: "It only takes one drink to get me steamboats. The problem is, I can't remember if it's the thirteenth or fourteenth."

Whisky may not cure the common cold, but it fails more agreeably than most other things.

Inspiring bold John Barleycorn!
What dangers thou canst make us scorn!
Wi' tipenny, we fear nae evil;
Wi' usquebae, we'll face the devil!
Robert Burns, honorary Glaswegian

'Have some wine,' the March Hare said in an encouraging tone. Alice looked around the table, but there was nothing on it but tea.

'I don't see any wine,' she remarked.

'There isn't any,' said the March Hare.

And that is why she nutted him, my Lord.

One evening in October, when I was one-third sober,
An' taking home a "load" with manly pride,
My poor feet began to stutter, so I lay down in the gutter,
And a pig came up an' lay down by my side.
Then we sang "It's all fair weather when good fellows
  get together,"
Till a lady passing by was heard to say:
"You can tell a man who boozes by the company he
  chooses."
And the pig got up and slowly walked away.

What's drinking? A pause from thinking.

There is nothing wrong with sobriety in moderation.

For a really bad hangover take two raw eggs and the
juice of a bottle of good malt whisky.

"I told the stewardess liquor for three."

"Who are the other two?"

"Oh, there are no other two."

               Sean Connery as James Bond

A night of good drinking is worth a year's thinking.

It's never really too early for a pint, is it?

Senga: "There comes a time in every woman's life when the only thing that helps is a bottle of Buckfast."

I'm only a common old working chap,
As anyone here can see,
But when I get a couple of drinks on a Saturday,
Glasgow belongs to me.
                    [*And me. I. B.*]

Wine is sunlight, held together by water.
                    Galileo Galilei

Shug: "I've never been drunk, but I've been over-served."

Be wary of strong drink. It can make you shoot at debt collectors – and miss.

Shug: "I decided to stop drinking with bampots and to drink only with friends. I've lost three stone."

Bacchus drowns within the bowl
Troubles that corrode the soul.
Horace. [No, not the one in The Broons]

No poems can live long or please that are written by water-drinkers.
Horace once again

They who drink beer will think beer.

Though a number of people have tried, no one has yet found a way to drink for a living.

Don't forget to stop and smell the hops.

There is one rapturous, wild, and ineffable pleasure – that of drinking at somebody else's expense.

Virgin Airlines have announced that their new giant double-decker plane has a private bar. A private bar? Is there a big problem with passengers from other planes stopping in for a drink?

People who drink at least have something to blame everything on.

Shug: "I drink to forget I drink."

The only way to have safe sex is to abstain. From drinking.

Senga: "I haven't touched a drop of alcohol since the invention of the funnel."

Shug: "Raindrops on roses and whiskers on kittens? Sod off. For me, it's enough beers while watching the football and getting so drunk I forget my name. These are a few of MY favourite things."

Ah, bottle, my friend, why do you empty yourself?

If your doctor warns that you have to watch your drinking, find a pub with a mirror.

Anybody that can't get drunk by midnight isn't really trying.

Alcohol, the cause of and solution to all of life's problems.
> *Says Homer Simpson, and who am I*
> *to gainsay a yellow-faced cartoon?*

An alcoholic is someone you don't like who drinks as much as you do.

Shug: "I don't have a drinking problem, except when I can't get one."

It is, of course, entirely possible to cook without using wine. It is also possible to wear undergarments made out of jute, but who wants to?

People are always willing to walk miles for a drink, but not for a bath.

Senga: "My grandfather is over ninety and he still doesn't need glasses. He drinks straight out of the bottle."

And our Biblical Section

A man hath no better thing under the sun, than to eat, and to drink, and to be merry.

Ecclesiastes

Give strong drink unto him that is ready to perish, and wine unto those that be of heavy hearts. Let him drink, and forget his poverty, and remember his misery no more.

Proverbs

A soft drink turneth away company.

It is only the first bottle that is expensive.

What whisky will not cure, there is no cure for.

They speak of my drinking, but never of my thirst.

Glasgow chat-up line
"I want a relationship that involves more than sex. Do you drink?"

You have had too much to drink if you feel sophisticated and can't pronounce it.

Not all men who drink are poets. Some of us drink because we aren't poets.

Had the earliest morality developed under the influence of beer, there would not be good or evil, there would be "kind of nice" or "pretty cool".
Frat boy in Buffy the Vampire Slayer

If you mean the demon drink that poisons the mind, pollutes the body, desecrates family life, and inflames sinners, then I'm against it. But if you mean the elixir of Christmas cheer, the shield against winter chill, the taxable potion that puts needed funds into public coffers to comfort little crippled children, then I'm for it. This is my position, and I will not compromise!

Any MSP

Senga: "I cook with wine. Sometimes I even put it in food."

In the good old days beer foamed and water from the tap didn't.

2
WIT OR WHIT?

Weegie Alzheimer's: you forget everything except the grudges.

Jimmie Macgregor, folk singer, broadcaster, hill-walker and West End boulevardier, tells this tale of his former mentor at Glasgow School of Art, Trevor Mackeson, a man who was as gay as the month of May during the times when it was dangerous to be so, and made no secret of it.

Jimmie was at the Close Theatre in Glasgow in the sixties, standing talking to Trevor in the bar, when they were suddenly assailed by what must have been one of the first dungareed, crop-haired feminists, a tiny woman who made up for her lack of inches by shouting. In this case she was shouting about equality in the home.

Trevor listened gravely until she petered out and then said, in that unmistakeable aristocratic camp drawl: "No, no, my dear. When a man returns from a hard day at the easel he wishes to find his wife draped invitingly across a *chaise longue*," and continued, looking loftily downward, "or in your case, a *chaise short*."

In a Glasgow night club, a former pop star and the one-time manager of Cowdenbeath sat drinking and recalling the days when they were well known.

Then, out of the blue, a beautiful blonde walked up to them, undid her blouse, took off her bra and wobbled her enormous boobs at them.

"I know you two," she said. "You had a hit in 1973 and you're the man who helped Cowdenbeath to the third round of the Scottish FA Cup. Can I have your autographs?" Flattered beyond belief, the two men got out their pens and two pieces of paper.

"No!" she protested, "I want you to sign my boobs!"

It was a strange request but she sat down between them and the has-beens went to work. The pop star tried desperately to sign her left boob but his pen skited along the soft white flesh, and the result was a splodgy mess.

The football manager, on the right hand boob, was having no trouble at all. He held her mammary firmly in his hand, and wrote his name in large letters using her nipple to dot the I. The pop star was puzzled.

"Hey, how come when I write on her boob, it all blots and runs, yet when you sign the other side, it comes out perfectly?" he asked.

The football supremo smiled. "That's easy," he replied. "You don't get to be the manager of Cowdenbeath without knowing how to sign right tits."

Many Glaswegians reckon that a job is an invasion of privacy.

A vain Glesga female goes to the beauty clinic and asks, "Whit is the secret of eternal youth?"

The wise beauty therapist tells her, "Bathe in milk every night."

The woman then asks, "Pasteurised or whit?"

"Naw," replies the therapist. "Up to your tits will dae."

Snow White is working away one morning when she hears a huge explosion. She quickly runs down to the mine where the seven dwarfs have been working.

To her horror she sees that the mine has collapsed. Frantically she screams, "Is anyone down there? Can anyone hear me?"

Silence.

She screams again, "Is anyone down there?"

All of a sudden she hears this hoarse voice croaking:

"Rangers are gonnae win the league."

Snow White says, "Thank God, at least Dopey is still alive."

3
GLASGOW RULES

No respect for a man who carries a dog. Not ever.
Never.

Don't ever say: "Can I ask you a question?" You
aren't really giving them a choice, are you? And that
can be dangerous.

A kind word is no substitute for a loaf. Nice, though.

Optimists are wrong just as often as pessimists, but
they have a better time.

A friend in need is a friend indeed. Except maybe in
Possil.

A wise man needs a hint. An eejit needs a doin'.

It's a great life if ye don't weaken.

Aye, okay, the world is a dangerous place. The trick
is no' to be feart.

A witty man may not be a wise one, but as sure as fuck he'll be clever.

A quote from the French revolutionary, Danton:
  'De l'audace, encore de l'audace, toujours de l'audace!'
Glaswegian translation:
  'Inty his mince, inty his mince again, never stoap gettin' inty his mince.'

"Dry yer eyes." This is defined in the Scottish Vernacular Dictionary as: "Instruction to another to cease and desist from whining and complaining. Often unrelated to any real tears. This is really a feckin cheeky thing to say, so make sure you are standing well away from the person to whom you say it . . .
  Example: "Aw, did wee diddums turn oot tae be HIV positive? Ach, dry yer eyes!"

Honest, it does say all of the above.

Glaswegian solution:
  The problem with people today is stupidity. I'm not saying there should be capital punishment for stupidity, but why don't we just take the safety labels off everything and let the problem solve itself?"

4
TALES TALL AND TRUE

This wee Glaswegian is at the doctor's complaining that he can't sleep at night and the doc asks him to talk him through an average day in his life to see if he can arrive at a diagnosis.

The guy starts: "Well, I usually get up about ten or so, have a couple of slices of toast, maybe with a poached egg, and start on the first bottle of voddy. I've usually polished that off by about one and then I start on the brandy with my lunch, usually some good healthy soup and a bit of fruit. The folks left me money and I don't need to work, so after I've finished the bottle of brandy I'll maybe take a wee walk through the park or down to the library."

The doctor is staring at him in amazement and says: "Go on."

The man says: "On the way back I'll get something for the tea and then get started on the whisky, usually Highland Park, while I'm eating it. Once that bottle is done in I go to the pub for a few hours, maybe a few nuts or crisps and half a dozen pints."

The doctor interrupts, saying in amazement, "Hold

on, you drink three bottles of spirits every day, followed by beer, and you say you can't get to sleep at night?"

"That's right, doc," smiles the chap. "I'm up all night singin' and dancin'."

On holiday in Jerusalem, a female journalist heard about an old Glasgow Jewish guy who had been going to the Western Wall (aka the Wailing Wall, though not to Jewish folk) during his holidays there, to pray, twice a day, every day, for a long, long time. So she went to check it out at the Western Wall.

She watches him pray and after about 45 minutes, when he turns to leave, she approaches him for an interview.

"I'm Shona Smith from BBC Scotland. How long have you been coming to the Western Wall and praying?"

"For about 50 years."

"50 years! That's amazing! What do you pray for?"

"I pray for peace between the Jews and the Arabs and for the Prods and Tims at home in Glasgow. I pray for all the hatred to stop and I pray for our children to grow up in safety and friendship."

"How do you feel after doing this for 50 years?"

"Like I'm talking to a fuckin' wall."

A Glaswegian marries for the first time. Three months later he meets his best man in the street.

"How's things, Sandy? Wife keeping ok?"

"No, she died, Harry."

"What happened?"

"Poisoned mushrooms."

"So sorry to hear that. My deepest sympathy, Sandy."

A year later our bold boy goes to the altar again, same best man, and another three months later they meet in the street by chance. Sandy informs Harry that his second wife has died too, same cause, poisoned mushrooms.

Another year goes by and our Sandy goes for wife number three. Harry (a right glutton for punishment, if you ask me) is again best man.

Three months later, another chance meeting on the street and the conversation goes something like this.

"Hi Sandy, how's the Mrs?"

"She died, Harry, she died. The week after the wedding this time."

"Aw, Sandy, surely not poisoned mushrooms again?"

"No, Harry. Short, sharp blow to the skull. Bitch wouldn't eat the poisoned mushrooms."

After a serious bomb attack in London, rescue workers found a girl, smothered in blood, alive in the rubble.

"Where are you bleeding from?" they asked.

"Brigton," said the girl. "But what the fuck huz that got tae dae wi' you?"

Wee Billy Ned from Maryhill always wanted to look cool. His friend told him that he needed a good designer pair of trainers to go with his shell suit. Billy saved up all his giros and all the money he got back from returning his empty bottles of Bucky and finally managed to get himself a pair of brilliant white trainers to go with his shell suit.

Proudly, he strutted down the street calling out to all the passers-by, "See ma new trainers? Cool, eh?" One fine upstanding gentleman pointed out that they were indeed a fine pair of trainers but was young Billy aware that he had a lace undone?

Billy scornfully retorted that it was part of being cool to have a trailing lace and that on the sole of the trainer there were instructions for the wearer to do such a thing. When asked for proof of this instruction, Billy took off his trainer and held it upside down for the disbeliever to read.

"There ye are! See, it says – Tai-wan."

A barmaid is advising a Weegie customer: "Don't drink any more. You're staggering."

The customer replies: "Is that right? Well, you're no bad-lookin' yersel."

5
PUBLIC NOTICES

F— F— F— Fuck it! Was That a Ferrari?

The Ferrari Formula One team fired their entire pit crew yesterday.

The announcement followed Ferrari's decision to take advantage of the UK Government's Youth Opportunity Scheme and employ people from Glasgow. The decision to hire them followed a recent documentary on how unemployed youths from the Govan and Possilpark areas of Glasgow were able to remove a set of wheels in less than 6 seconds without proper equipment, whereas Ferrari's existing crew take 8 seconds to do it despite having millions of euros worth of high-tech gear.

Prime Minister Tony Blair went on record as saying this was a bold move by the Ferrari management, which demonstrated the international recognition of the UK under New Labour – as he would, the fascist sook.

As most races are won and lost in the pits, Ferrari thought they had the advantage over every other team. However, Ferrari, as you might expect if you have read this far, got more than they bargained for.

At the first practise session, the Govan & Possilpark pit crew successfully changed the tyres in less than 6 seconds, but within 12 seconds of laying hands on the car they had resprayed it, rebadged it, and sold it to the McLaren team for eight bottles of Stella, two ounces of dope, a bunch of those cool trackies the pit guys wear and some photos of Coulthard's burd in the shower.

Urgent – Earthquake Appeal

At 00.54 on Friday 30 November 2006 a major earthquake hit, measuring 4.8 on the Richter Scale and epicentred in Glasgow.

Victims were seen wandering aimlessly, muttering, "Ah wiz shiteing masel," and, "Ah need a fag and a Cally Special". The earthquake decimated the area, causing almost £30 worth of damage, with the exception of the Dalmarnock Area, where approximately £375,000 of improvements were made.

Untold disruption and distress was caused. Many were woken well before their Giro arrived. Several priceless collections of mementoes from the Balearics and Spanish Costas were damaged. Three areas of historical and scientifically significant litter were disturbed.

The cone fell off the head of the statue of the Duke of Wellington outside the Gallery of Modern Art. The one on his horse, Copenhagen, managed to remain on the horse's head, albeit at a jaunty angle. Thousands are confused and bewildered, trying to come to terms with the fact that something interesting has happened in Glasgow.

One resident, Mary-Alice McGregor, a 17-year-old mother of three, said: "It was such a shock, my little Chelsea came running into my bedroom crying. My youngest two, Tyler-Morgan and Shania, slept through it all. I was still shaking when I was watching *Trisha* the next morning."

Apparently though, looting did carry on as normal. The British Red Cross have, so far, managed to ship 4,000 crates of Buckfast Tonic Wine to the area to help the stricken masses. Rescue workers are still searching through the rubble and have found large quantities of personal belongings including benefit books and jewellery from Elizabeth Duke at Argos.

HOW YOU CAN HELP

Clothing is most sought after. Items required include:

Sovvy Rings

Baseball caps

Shell suits

Tesco two-stripe trainers

White socks
Chunky gold chains

Food parcels may be harder to put together but are necessary all the same. Required foodstuffs include:
Frozen burgers
Buckfast
Deep fried Mars Bars
Buckfast
Golden Wonder Crisps (prawn cocktail)
Buckfast
Square Sausage wi broon sauce
Buckfast
Chips and curry sauce
Buckfast
Black, white or fruit pudding
Buckfast
Fray Bentos Steak & Kidney Pies
Olde English cider
Buckfast
Lard
Ready cut frozen chips
Buckfast

PLEASE SEND A DONATION

– £2.00 buys chips, scraps and a bottle of ginger, preferably Dunn's or Alpine Iron Brew, for a family of four.

– 22 pence buys a biro for filling in spurious compensation claims.

– £1.95 buys an all-day bus pass to enable disaster victims to travel between the Social, the Posty, the Offy, McDonald's, What Everys and Glasgow Green or Elder Park for the refugees' garden party.

Please send your credit card number and a sample signature.

Thank you.

*

Three of four associates of Bin Laden were arrested in Easterhouse last night – Bin Robbing, Bin Dealing, and Bin Fighting. They are still looking for Bin Working.

Overheard on a bus:

"Ah'm no sayin it's a rough pub, but if the bouncer frisks ye an disny find a chib, he gies ye wan."

Comparisons

Moscovites will consume marinated mushrooms and vodka, salted herring and vodka, smoked salmon and vodka, salami and vodka, caviar on brown bread and vodka, pickled cucumbers and vodka, cold tongue and vodka, beetroot salad and vodka, onions and vodka – anything and everything and vodka.

So how do you tell them from Weegies?

6
BUS PASS CORNER

It's Sunday night in Glasgow and the 93-year-old is getting spiffed up for the evening. He's got the good blue suit on, big, loud American tie from the forties, shoes so polished you can see your face in them, nails neatly trimmed, face shaved to shininess. What's left of his hair is combed sideways, parting arrow-straight.

He goes into a hotel bar and finds a stool next to this nice woman. She's in her mid-80's, blue hair, pearls, cocktail dress, the whole thing. He asks her, "Is that a Martini you're drinking?"

She smiles pleasantly and nods.

"Would you like another?" Another smile and nod. He signs to the barman, who puts one in front of each of them. He takes a sip, and turns to her. "So tell me," he says, "do I come here often?"

A nice couple from the Garngad are in their nineties and are having problems remembering things. They decide to go to the doctor for a check-up. The doctor tells them that they are physically okay, but they might want to start writing things down to help them remember.

Later that night, while watching TV, the old guy gets up from his chair. His wife asks, "Where are you going?"

He says, "To the kitchen."

"Will you get me some of that ice cream?"

"Aye," he replies.

"Don't you think you should write it down so you can remember it?"

"No, I can remember it."

"Well, I'd like some strawberries on top. You'd better write it down cos you know you'll forget it."

He says, "I can remember that! You want a bowl of ice cream with strawberries."

"I'd like some of that whipped cream with the brandy in it as well. I'm certain you'll forget that, so you'd better write it down."

Irritated, he says, "I don't need to write it down. I can remember it. Leave me alone. Ice cream with strawberries and whipped cream for Goad sakes!" Then he grumbles off into the kitchen.

After about twenty minutes the old man returns from the kitchen and hands his wife a plate of bacon and eggs.

She stares at the plate for a moment and then says, "Nae breid?"

Eighty-year-old Bessie bursts into the telly room at the retirement home. She holds her clenched fist in the air and announces, "Anyone who can guess what's in my hand can have sex with me tonight." An elderly gent in the rear shouts out, "An elephant?" Bessie thinks for a minute and says, "That's close enough."

This woman from Partick goes to a new dentist. His name seems familiar, but he's fat and old and bald, so she decides she doesn't know him. Then after a while she asks him the Glasgow question – what school he went to. He tells her. Same school as her. She asks him what year he left. Same year. She says to him, "You know, I think you were in my class."

"Oh aye," he says, "what did you teach?"

OLD IS WHEN . . .

Your friends compliment you on your new alligator shoes and you are not wearing shoes or socks.

A sexy burd catches your eye and your pacemaker starts the car.

Going bra-less means that your face is wrinkle-free.

You don't care where your spouse goes, just as long as you don't have to go too.

You are cautioned to slow down by the doctor instead of by the polis.

"Getting a wee bit of action" means there's no need for the All-Bran today.

"Getting lucky" means finding your house first time.

An "all-nighter" means not getting up to go to the toilet.

Nostalgia. Do you remember the first time you heard the word?

Decisions were made by going, "eeny-meeny-miney-mo."

"Race issues" meant arguing about who ran the fastest.

"Money issues" were handled by whoever was the banker in Monopoly.

Catching moths could happily occupy an entire evening.

It wasn't odd to have two or three "best" friends.

Being old referred to anyone over twenty.

The net on a tennis court was the perfect height to play volleyball and rules didn't matter.

The worst thing you could catch from the opposite sex was measles.

It was magic when your dad would "remove" his thumb.

It was unbelievable that dodgieball wasn't an Olympic event.

Having a weapon at school meant being caught with a sling.

Nobody was nicer-looking than your Mammy.

Scrapes and bruises were kissed and made better.

Getting a foot of snow was a dream come true.

Abilities were discovered because of "ah double dare ye."

Saturday morning cartoons weren't thirty-minute ads for action figures.

Spinning around, getting dizzy and falling down was a good reason for laughing.

The worst embarrassment was being picked last for a team.

War was a card game.

Water pistols were the ultimate weapon.

A bit of card in the spokes transformed any bike into a motorcycle.

Taking drugs meant aspirin.

Ice cream was considered a basic food group.

Older siblings were the worst tormentors, but also the fiercest protectors.

7
AN APOLOGY
AND THREE REALLY FUNNY SONGS

In a book I did, the sequel to *Weegies vs Edinbuggers/ Edinbuggers vs Weegies* titled, with that vaulting leap of the imagination for which I am renowned, *Merr Weegies vs Edinbuggers/Mair Edinbuggers vs Weegies*, I used a couple of songs which I culled from a website, with the owner's permission. What I did not know was that the owner had blagged said songs without permission from somewhere else. The author of these songs is an extremely pleasant guy called Mark Rafferty.

He contacted the publisher, asking, with only the tiniest degree of miffedness, why I had used his songs without his permission. What he didn't know at the time was that I was singing his songs in the *Uisge Beatha,* the pub in Woodlands Road, on Sunday evenings.

I emailed him with a grovelling apology, gracefully accepted, and we met for a coffee. Not my choice – Mark doesn't drink and he is a counsellor of alcoholics in Greenock, not the ideal place for a St Mirren fan, which is what he is, a serious one.

Part of the deal we struck was that I would say, in big letters:

St. Mirren are the best team in the world and the Old Firm are a bunch of total fandans.

Happy to do so and I agree, as it happens, with the second part. Here are the songs, plus a new one, part, I think you'll agree, of Weegie wit and wisdom.

DEDICATED FOLLOWER OF RANGERS

Tune: Dedicated Follower of Fashion

His teeth are green, his head is square,
Wi' a big moustache, and curly hair.
One day he's on Paisley Road, the next day he's in
    jail.
He's a dedicated follower of Rangers.

He hates the Tims, he loves the Queen
A naked burd, he's never seen.
He holidays in Airdrie and his breath would make
ye scream.
He's a dedicated follower of Rangers.

He likes to sing: "Hello, Hello"
He likes to drink . . . El Dor-a-do.
There's one thing that he hates and that is
cleanliness.
He thinks that Derek Johnstone is a handsome,
witty man.
He's a dedicated follower of Rangers.

His team get gubbed in a foreign land,
And once again, he's on remand,
But he knows a real good lawyer from his local
marching band.
He's a dedicated follower of Rangers.

He bangs the drum . . . in Motherwell.
He bares the bum . . . ootside chap-el.
He'd probably be a champ if being a fanny was a
sport.
He's a dedicated follower of Rangers.

WHERE EVERYBODY KNOWS YOUR GAME

Tune: Where Everybody Knows Your Name

Making your way in Europe today
    takes everything you've got.
Sixty thousand diddies wi' season tickets bought,
But mebbe ye huv tae win a game,
In order to progress,
A bit beyond the second round,
Where bams like you are never found.
It's just another fact of life.
It's never gonny go away.
There's nae Tims left in Europe on Christmas Day.

It's a grand old team to play for,
    or so we're fucking told.
Yet every year in Europe there's eleven jerseys sold.
Tae hasbeen shites fae France or Spain,
Who just can't believe their luck,
When yer name comes oot the hat,
Tae cries of: "Who the fuck is that?"
You're just a pishy Glasgow team.
You gie us a' the boke.
Yer European campaign's a fucking joke.

THE GIRO SONG

Tune: The Sound of Silence

Hello Giro my old friend, I've come to cash you in again,

Cos Tony Blair pays us fortnightly, 107 pounds and ninety pee

And the Post Office they will cash it in for free – just you see

Wur goin round . . . tae Haddows.

And when those housing cheques they come

Wur gonnae cash them one by one,

Huvnae had a housing cheque for weeks . . .

The flat's a tip and the kitchen reeks . . .

And the cider drinking's only just begun . . .

Ice Dragon,

Wur goin round . . . tae Haddows.

And when my giro comes tae me, am gonnae spend it sensiblee . . .

My weekly shopping is a wonderful sight,

A crate of Bucky and a Turkish Delight . . .

And a bar of soap, just in case I ever find romance

Fat fucking chance,

Wur goin round . . . tae Haddows.

But now my cash has all been blown, it's time to
    get a crisis loan,
Ma story's ready and its aff tae the Bru,
"Ah need some shoes av got an interview",
Wi a pair of boots, I'll be working by tomorrow
    night,
That'll be right,
Wur goin round . . . tae Haddows.

And in my tenement flat I saw, ten outright wasters
    maybe more . . .
People drinking without speaking
Taking bevvy without asking
Either signing on, or claiming incapacity,
Just like me,
Wur goin round . . . tae Haddows.

Repeat first verse to finish

Mark has a CD available for sale, and these songs are
on it, plus others equally funny. Try his website
www.myspace.com/markrafferty, which has mp3s of his
comedy tunes plus gig info etc. He plays live a lot
under the pseudonym "mr mark" and is worth looking
out for.

8
EVERYBODY MUST GET STONED

There is an oft-quoted statistic about the Eskimos having thirty-one words for snow, usually brought forth as though it was unusual or amazing. The Eskimos may know a lot about snow, but have you ever tried to tot up the number of words Glaswegians use for being inebriated?

The following is the result of a poll one evening in the pub. There are bound to be a lot more, so I've left a space at the end for you to add your own.

What does this say of our society, I wonder.

My own favourite is: "At peace with the floor." But did you know that we have been using the word "fou" for this condition since the 1500s?

Don't even start to think about the number of Glasgow words for bampot . . .

A couple of chapters into the novel (I think that this may only be used by people in the Doublet Bar in Glasgow's West End)

Arseholed

Banjaxed

Bent

Bladdered

Blitzed

Blitzkrieged

Blootered

Blotto

Bombed

Buzzed

Derailed

Embalmed

Fermented

Floatin'

Fou as a coo

Fou as a piper

Fou as a wulk

Fou as Betty

Fucked

Fucked up

Gassed

Had a skinful

Hammered

Happy

High as a kite
(and many other things, including the 4th of July)

Hummin'

Influenced

In rare form

Intoxicated

Jazzed

Jiggered

Just south of bejesus

Knackered (aka cream-crackered)

KO'd

Legless

Liquored up

Lit

Lit up

Loaded

Lubed

Lushed

Marinated

Mortal

Mingin'

Miroc

Miroculous

Muntit

Off his face

Off his nut

Oot ae it

Out of his tree

Pickled

Pie-eyed

Pished

Pished out his face

Pissed

Pissed as a newt (and dozens of other things, including a lottery winner)

Pixelated

Plastered

Polluted

Rat-arsed

Reekin'

Ripped

Saturated

Sauced

Scuppered

Shellacked

Shickered

Shit-faced

Shithoused

Slammed

Sloshed

Smashed

Soused

Spongy (from Macbeth, I'm told. Erudite lot in the Doublet)

Squiffy

Spifflicated

Steamboats

Steamin'

Stewed

Stoned

Stupefied

Tanked

Three sheets to the wind

Tied one on

Tight

Tipsy

Tired and emotional

Toasted

Trashed

Under the affluence

Under the weather

Unsober

Wasted

Wellied

Well-oiled

Wrecked

Zonked

Here is the space for you to put in the ones that I
have missed out:

9
THREATS AND INSULTS

Both of the above are Weegie specialties. Here are a few of the less vicious ones.

Glaswegian comment on our national instrument: "The best thing that you can say about bagpipes is that they don't fucking smell too."

Weegies do put-downs better than anybody

He, she or you has a:

    face like a painter's radio

    face like a bucket of smashed crabs

    face like a bulldog licking piss off a stinging nettle

    face like a dropped meat pie

    face like a fox licking shit off a thistle

    face only a mother could love

    face that would scare a dog out of a butcher shop

    face like a par 3 tee box

face like a smacked arse

face like a tub of fire-damaged Lego

face like a bag of spanners

face like a chewed caramel

face like a bulldog chowin' a waasp. (Always with both a's.)

face like a burst couch

face like a burst tomato

face like a melted welly

face like a well-skelped arse

face like it went on fire and somebody put the flames out with a shovel

face like the back o' a bus

face like the back o' the lum

face like a bashed thrup'ny bit (For oldsters only. An old-money threepenny coin was 12-sided.)

face like a burst settee

face like a burst melodeon

face like a flittin'

face that would drive rats from a barn

face like a bag o' bruised fruit

face like a hen layin razors

face like a saft tattie

face like a skittery nappy

face like a picture – it needs hanging

face like a torn scone

face like a wet washing

face like a weel-kickit ba'

face like a wet nicht lookin' for a dry mornin'

face that has worn oot three boadies.

face ye'd never get tired kickin'

face like a chipped chanty

face like a German bank – fou o' marks

face like a fish supper – fou o' chips

a rerr face fur hauntin' hooses

a heid like a clootie dumplin'

face thit wid get a piece it any door

face like a Hallowe'en cake

face is like a bookie's poakit – full o' lines!

*A few other random insults, threats and thoughts
to use on suitable occasions*

She walks like she's goat two legs in the wan knicker!

I can only please one person a day. Today is not your day. Tomorrow doesn't look good either.

Arsehole is not an alternative lifestyle.

The male chromosome, particularly in Glaswegians, is an incomplete female chromosome. In other words, the male is a walking abortion, aborted at the gene stage.
   To be male is to be deficient, emotionally limited; maleness is a deficiency disease and males are emotional cripples.
   And your point is, madam?
   Don't you sometimes wish that Adam had died in full possession of all of his ribs?

If you can't live without me, why aren't you dead?

I feel so miserable without you, it's almost like having you here.

I like long walks, especially when they are taken by you. Now!

Sometimes I need what only you can provide: your absence.

You're a good example of why some animals eat their young.

Don't look now, but there's one too many in this room and I think it's you.

Every time I look at you I get a burning need to be lonely.

Describe you? This is the bit where we get out the thesaurus and look up synonyms for "arsehole".

Your mother should have thrown you away and kept the stork.

10
SOME FACTS ABOUT YOU, WEEGIE HEID

1) You will never play professional basketball.

2) You swear very well.

3) At least one of your cousins holds political office.

4) You think you sing very well.

5) You have no idea how to make a long story short.

6) You can talk about football for 72 hours straight.

7) There isn't a huge difference between losing your temper and killing someone.

8) Much of your food is boiled.

9) You have never hit your head on the ceiling.

10) You spent a good portion of your childhood inside.

11) You're strangely poetic after a few beers.

12) You are, therefore, poetic a lot.

13) You will be punched for no good reason – a lot.

14) Some punches directed at you are legacies from past generations.

15) Your sister will punch you because your brother punched her.

16) Many of your sisters are Catherine, Elizabeth or Mary – and one is Mary Catherine Elizabeth.

17) Someone in your family is incredibly cheap. It is more than likely you.

18) You may not know the words, but that doesn't stop you from singing.

19) You can't wait for the other guy to stop talking so you can start talking.

20) "Mix'n'macs" is a euphemism for "fried leftovers from the fridge".

21) You're not nearly as funny as you think you are, but what you lack in talent you make up for in frequency.

22) There wasn't a huge difference between your last funeral and your last keg party.

23) You are, or know someone, named "Jimmy".

24) If you don't know Jimmy, then you know Mac, if you don't know Jimmy or Mac, then you know Wullie, and you'll probably also know Wullie MacJimmy.

25) You are genetically incapable of keeping a secret.

26) Your parents were on a first name basis with everyone at the local emergency room.

27) And last but not least . . . Being a Weegie means . . . your attention span is so short that . . . oh, forget it.

11
POSSIBLY THE WORST STORY
EVER TOLD

A Weegie is driving down the road and breaks down near a Buddhist monastery in the Borders. He goes to the monastery, knocks on the door, and says, "My car broke down. Do you think that I could stay the night?" The monks graciously accept him, feed him dinner, even fix his car.

As the man tries to fall asleep, he hears a strange sound. The next morning, he asks the monks what the sound was, but they say, "We can't tell you. You're not a monk."

The man is disappointed but thanks them anyway and goes on his merry way.

Some years later, the same man breaks down in front of the same monastery.

The monks again accept him, feed him, even fix his car. That night, he hears the same strange noise that he had heard years earlier. The next morning, he asks what it is, but the monks reply, "We can't tell you. You're not a monk."

The man says, "All right, all right. I'm dying to know. If the only way I can find out what that sound was is to become a monk, how do I become a monk?"

The monks reply, "You must travel the earth and tell us how many blades of grass there are. When you find this number, you will become a monk."

The man sets about his task. Some forty-five years later, he returns and knocks on the door of the monastery. He says, "I have travelled the earth and have found what you have asked for. There are 145,236,284,232 blades of grass on the earth."

The monks reply, "Congratulations. You are now a monk. We shall now show you the way to the sound."

The monks lead the man to a wooden door, where the head monk says, "The sound is right behind that door."

The man reaches for the knob, but the door is locked. He says, "Aye, very funny. May I have the key?"

The monks give him the key, and he opens the door. Behind the wooden door is another door made of stone. The man demands the key to the stone door. The monks give him the key, and he opens it, only to find a door made of ruby.

He demands another key from the monks, who provide it. Behind that door is another door, this one made of sapphire. So it went until the man had gone through doors of emerald, silver, topaz, and amethyst.

Finally, the monks say: "This is the last key to the last door."

The man is relieved and unlocks the door, turns the knob, and behind that door he is amazed to find the source of that strange sound.

But I can't tell you what it is, because you're not a monk.

Or could this one be the worst story ever told?

A Glaswegian walks into a restaurant with a full-grown ostrich behind him. The waitress asks for their orders. The man says, "A hamburger, chips and a coke," and turns to the ostrich, "What's yours?"

"I'll have the same," says the ostrich.

A short time later the waitress returns with the order. "That will be £9.40 please," she says and the man reaches into his pocket and pulls out the exact amount for payment.

The next day, the man and the ostrich come again and the man says, "A hamburger, chips, and a coke." The ostrich says, "I'll have the same." Again the man reaches into his pocket and pays with the exact amount.

For a while this becomes routine until the two enter again later in the week. "The usual?" asks the waitress.

"No, this time it's a treat, so I will have a steak, a baked potato, and a salad," says the man.

"Yes! Same for me," says the ostrich.

Shortly the waitress brings the order and says, "That will be £32.62."

Once again the man pulls the exact amount out of his pocket and places it on the table.

The waitress can't hold back her curiosity any longer. "Excuse me. How do you manage to always come up with the exact money from your pocket every time?"

"Well," says the man, "several years ago I was clearing the attic and found an old lamp. When I rubbed it a genie appeared and offered me two wishes. My first wish was that if I ever had to pay for anything, I would just put my hand in my pocket and the right amount of money would always be there."

"That's brilliant," says the waitress. "Most people would wish for a couple of million pounds or something, but you'll always be as rich as you want for as long as you live."

"That's right. Whether it's a pint of milk or a Rolls Royce, the exact money is always there," says the guy.

The waitress asks, "But what is all this aboot with the ostrich?" The man sighs, pauses, and replies, "My second wish was for a tall burd with a big arse and long legs who agrees with everything I say."

Or this one?

A Glasgow company is developing computer chips that store music in women's breast implants. This is being considered a major breakthrough and will solve a perennial problem.

The perennial problem:

Women are always complaining about men staring at their breasts and not listening to them.

A Glaswegian met a beautiful blonde lady and decided he wanted to marry her right away.

She said, "But we don't know anything about each other."

He said, "That's all right, we'll learn about each other as we go along."

So she consented, they were married, and off they went on a honeymoon at a very nice resort.

One morning they were lying by the pool when he got up off his towel, climbed up to the ten metre diving board, did a two and a half tuck, followed by three rotations in the pike position, straightened out and cut the water like a knife. After a few more demonstrations, he came back and lay back down on the towel.

She said, "That was incredible!"

He said, "I used to be an Olympic diving champion. You see, I told you we'd learn more about each other as we went along."

So she got up, jumped into the pool, and started doing laps. After seventy-five laps, she climbed out of the pool, lay down on her towel, and was hardly out of breath.

He said, "That was incredible! Were you an Olympic endurance swimmer?"

"No," she replied, "I was a prostitute in Greenock, but I worked both sides of the river."

12
THE ANTI-EDINBUGGER ONE

You didn't think that you were going to get a book called *Weegie Wit and Wisdom* without a few snidies about the Eastcoasters, did you? So here we go . . .

Are you normally this unpleasant, or are you just having an Edinbugger moment?

Wullie the Weegie had just had a medical check up. "I hate to be the one to break it to you," said the doctor, "but you've only got about 6 months to live."

"Oh my God," gasped Wullie, turning white.

A few minutes later, after the news had sunk in, Wullie said, "Doctor, you've known me a long time. Do you have any suggestions as to how I could make the most of my remaining months?"

"Have you ever married?" asked the doctor.

Wullie replied that he had been a bachelor his whole life.

"You might think about taking a wife," said the doctor, "after all, you'll need someone to look after you during the final illness."

"That's a good point," said Wullie, "and with only six months to live I better make the most of my remaining time."

"May I make one more suggestion?" asked the doctor. "Marry an Edinburgh girl."

"An Edinburgh girl? Why?" asked Wullie.

"It'll seem longer."

There are only two kinds of people in the world – Glaswegians, and those who wish they were.

The Edinbuggers have perfected good manners and made them indistinguishable from rudeness.

Some Edinbuggers are born mediocre, some Edinbuggers achieve mediocrity, and some Edinbuggers have mediocrity thrust upon them.

An Edinbugger never hurts anyone's feelings unintentionally.

An Edinbugger is as good as his word – and his word is no good.

Weegies cause happiness wherever they go; Edinbuggers, whenever they go.

13

WEEGIE AS SHE IS SPOKE

In Glasgow a new form of rhyming slang has developed – one that uses our own pronunciation. Eg:

"Are ye corned?" I said. "Sit doon on yer chorus and we'll have a wee Salvador. Mine's a Mick by the way."

'Corned' is short for 'corned beef', as in 'deef'; 'chorus' is from 'chorus and verse', rhyming with erse; 'Salvador', as in 'Dali', rhymes with 'swally'; 'Mick' of course means lager.

There are dozens of these, but it is more fun to make up your own: 'Denis Law' = 'snaw', for example. And what would the temperature be like if it was Bertie Auld?

Here is a wee space for you to insert your own:

14
DOWN BY LAW: MINGERS AND MORONS

A very worrying load of information. Can you imagine working for a company that has a little more than 500 employees and has the following statistics? At time of writing:

29 have been accused of spouse abuse

7 have been arrested for fraud

19 have been accused of writing bad cheques

117 have directly or indirectly bankrupted at least 2 businesses

3 have done time for assault

71 cannot get a credit card due to bad credit

14 have been arrested on drug-related charges

8 have been arrested for shoplifting

21 are currently defendants in lawsuits

84 have been arrested for drunk driving in the last year

Can you guess which organization this is? Yep, it's the 646 members of the Houses of Parliament. The same group that cranks out hundreds of new laws each year designed to keep the rest of us in line.

15
MORE TALES TALL AND TRUE

Senga tells Shug, "You're an eejit! You always were an eejit and you always will be a eejit! You look, act and dress like an eejit! You'll be an eejit until the day you die! And if they ran a world-wide competition for eejits, you would be the world's second biggest eejit!"

"Why only second place?" Shug asks.

"Because you're an eejit!" Senga screams.

What did the waiter ask the group of Milngavie matrons?

"Is anything OK?"

An Archbishop and a Glasgow taxi driver died on the same day. When they got to the Pearly Gates they were met by Saint Peter, whom they asked for entry into Paradise.

Saint Peter checked his files.

He said to the taxi driver, "Here, take this golden staff and silk robe and enter into the Kingdom of Heaven."

Saint Peter turned to the Archbishop and said, "Take this thin cotton robe and a wooden staff and enter into the Kingdom of Heaven."

The Archbishop was very annoyed and he questioned Saint Peter. "Don't you think you have us mixed up, Saint Peter?"

"Don't think so, pal," said Saint Peter. "When you preached, everybody slept. And when the taxi driver drove, everybody prayed."

Another true story is of the young man coming down the street singing: "Twenty-one today; twenty-one today". A passer-by inquires, in innocence, if it's the chap's 21st birthday. The young man proceeds to malky the enquirer then skips away singing, "Twenty-two today".

This wee Weegie walks up to a woman in his office and tells her that her hair smells nice.

The woman immediately goes in to her supervisor's office and tells him that she wants to file a sexual harassment suit and explains why.

The supervisor is puzzled by this and says, "What's wrong with a guy telling you your hair smells nice?"

The woman replies, "He's a midget."

A tiny but dignified old Weegie wumman was among a group looking at an art exhibition in a newly opened gallery. Suddenly one contemporary painting caught her eye.

"What the fuck," she inquired of the artist standing nearby, "is that?"

He smiled condescendingly. "That, missus, is supposed to be a mother and her child."

"Well then," snapped the wee Weegie wumman, "why isn't it?"

Davie received a very Weegie parrot for his birthday. This parrot was fully grown with a bad attitude and worse vocabulary. Every other word was an expletive. Those that weren't expletives were, to say the least, very rude indeed, with "fannybaws" and "minger" the least of them.

Davie tried hard to change the bird's attitude and was constantly saying polite words, playing soft music, anything that came to mind. Nothing worked. He yelled at the bird, the bird got worse. He shook the bird and the bird got madder and ruder.

Finally, in a moment of desperation, Davie put the parrot in the freezer. For a few moments he heard the bird squawking, kicking and screaming and then, suddenly, all was quiet.

Davie was frightened that he might have actually

hurt the bird and quickly opened the freezer door. The parrot calmly stepped out on to David's extended arm and said: "I'm sorry that I offended you with my language and actions. I ask for your forgiveness. I will try to check my behaviour and keep the language down."

Davie was astounded at the bird's change in attitude and was about to ask what changed him when the parrot continued, "Might I ask what the chicken did?"

A man was watching a woman in the supermarket with a three-year-old girl in her trolley. As they passed the biscuit aisle, the wee girl asked for a biscuit and her mother told her, "No." The little girl immediately began to whine and girn, and the mother said quietly, "Now, Monica, we just have half of the aisles left to go through – don't be upset. It won't be long now."

Soon, they came to the sweetie aisle and the little girl began to shout for sweeties. When told she couldn't have any, she began to cry. The mother said, "There, there, Monica, don't cry – only two more aisles to go and then we'll be checking out."

When they got to the checkout, the moppet immediately began to clamour for chewing gum and burst into a terrible tantrum upon discovering there'd be no gum purchased. The mother said serenely,

"Monica, we'll be through this checkout in five minutes and then you can go home and have a nice nap."

A man followed them out to the car park and stopped the woman to compliment her. "I couldn't help noticing how patient you were with little Monica," he began.

The mother replied, "Her name is Kelly-Marie. I'm Monica."

Aunt Matilda lives in Milngavie and is a very proper lady. During Easter her 10-year-old nephew, Joe, from Possil, came to visit and they took a walk through the streets of Milngavie. As they were walking, a bow-legged old man came by and Joe said: "Shit! Look at his legs. What the fuck is wrong with him?"

Aunt Matilda was shocked by his swearing and replied, "Now, Joe, maybe in Possil you might get by with talking like that but not here in Milngavie. We have manners here and you will too!"

They stopped at a cafe and were sitting at a table when another bow-legged bloke came by. Joe saw him and said, "Jesus Christ! There's another one!"

That was all that Aunt Matilda could stand. She decided to take Joe to the library to spend the day with her librarian friend, Gertrude. Joe was to study Shakespeare all day in order to teach him to speak properly.

That night, after the library had closed, Aunt Matilda and Joe were walking home. Sure enough, another bow-legged man passed by. Aunt Matilda held her breath, wondering what Joe would say.

Joe looked at the bandy guy then looked up at Aunt Matilda and said, "Behold! What manner of men are these, they that carry their balls in parentheses?"

A Weegie vampire bat came flapping in from the night covered in fresh blood and parked himself on the roof of the cave to get some sleep. Soon all the other bats smelled the blood and began harassing him about where he got it. He told them to go away and let him get some sleep but they persisted – "Tell us! Gonny, gonny, gonny?" – until finally he gave in.

"OK, follow me," he said and flew out of the cave with hundreds of bats behind him.

Down through the Clyde valley they went, across the river and into a forest. Finally he slowed down and all the other bats excitedly milled around him. "Now, do you see that tree over there?" he asked.

"Aye, aye, aye. We see it! We see it!" the bats all screamed in a frenzy.

"Good," said the first bat, "because Ah didnae."

16
SEE INSULTS? SEE US?
SEE COLOURFUL?

Here are some oldies and goldies with the odd new one thrown in just for practice:

Him, he's much use as a one legged man in an arse-kicking competition

She's dressed up like a dog's dinner

He's about as useful as a condom machine in the Vatican

She's been up and down more times than a whore's drawers

She's been engaged more times than a telephone switchboard

He's tighter than a photo finish

Daz wouldn't shift her

He thinks manual labour is a Spanish musician

He's as funny as a burning orphanage

He's got a head balder than a baby's arse

He's got the dress sense of an Oxfam model

Not even the tide would take her out

Mother Teresa wouldn't kiss her

He's got a nose like a blind carpenter's thumb

Last time I saw a face like that it had a noose round it

He's so camp he shites tent pegs

I'm as sick as a plane to Lourdes

He's as much use as a trapdoor on a lifeboat

She's colder than a penguin's bollocks

SEE INSULTS? SEE US? SEE COLOURFUL?

She's had more pricks than a second hand dartboard

I've seen better teeth on a worn-out gearbox

She's no show pony but she would do for a ride around the house

She's so easy to pick up they call her BBC1

He's as useful as a grave robber in a crematorium

Whiter than a pair of Snow White's knickers

About as innocent as a nun doing press-ups in a cucumber field

They've got a picture of her at the hospital – it saves using the stomach pump

I'm so hungry I'd eat a scabby-heided wean

You're as welcome as a fart in a spacesuit

He has rubber-lined pockets so he can steal soup

As busy as the Easterhouse dole

Sweating like a paedophile

As tight as a nun's knickers

I'm so horny I'd get up the crack of dawn

Did your mother find out who your father is yet?

Jesus, she could breastfeed a creche

A sniper wouldn't take her out

I wouldn't ride that one into battle

She wouldn't get a kick in a stampede

Does your train of thought ever have a guard van?

Every now and then you meet someone whose ignorance is encyclopedic.

When God was handing out personalities, you must have been holding the door.

You're so boring even a boomerang wouldn't come back to you.

Why don't you go and get lost somewhere where they don't have a "found" department?

I'm busy trying to imagine you with a personality. Maybe you'd be less boring once I got to know you, but I don't want to take that chance.

Looking at you, Darwin would not be pleased

Why don't you put your glasses on backwards and walk into yourself, you shonky-arsed, sister-shagging, armpit-licking, tit-sucking, haemorrhoid-nibbling, wank-brained fuckwit!

And we do have some surreal expressions of disbelief

Yer arse in parsley!

Your bum's oot the windae

Yer ba's are a' beef

And then yer arse fell aff

17

MELODIC MEMORIES

Some daft songs from the past, back when Gary Glitter was still a fine upstanding member of the rock and roll community. I've never heard them sung outside Glasgow.

THERE IS A HAPPY LAND

There is a happy land, down in Duke Street Jail,
Where all the prisoners stand, tied tae a nail.
Ham and eggs they never see, durty watter fur
    their tea,
There they live in miser-ee,
"God save the Queen".

YE CANNY SHOVE YER GRANNY AFF A BUS

Oh! ye canny shove yer granny aff a bus,
Ye canny shove yer granny aff a bus.
Ye canny shove yer granny,
Coz she's yer mammy's mammy,

Ye canny shove yer granny aff a bus.

Ye can shove yer ither granny aff a bus,
Ye can shove yir ither granny aff a bus.
Ye can shove yir ither granny,
Coz she's yer daddy's mammy,
Ye can shove this ither granny aff a bus.

OH DEAR, WHAT CAN THE MATTER BE?

Oh dear, what can the matter be?
Six old ladies got stuck in the lavatory
They were there from Sunday to Saturday
And nobody knew they were there.

The first to come in was old Mrs Flynn
She prided herself on being so thin
But when she sat down, the poor dear fell in
And nobody knew she was there.

CHORUS

The next to come in was old Mrs Bender
She wanted to fix up a broken suspender
It snapped and injured her feminine gender
And nobody knew she was there.

CHORUS

The third to come in was old Mrs Humphrey
When she sat down she found it quite comfy
She tried to get up but could not get her bum free
And nobody knew she was there.

CHORUS

The fourth to come in was old Mrs Brewster
She couldn't see as well as she used to
Sat on the handle, swore someone had goosed her
And nobody knew she was there.

CHORUS

The next to go in was young Mrs Slaughter
She was the Duke of Effingham's daughter.
She went there to pass off superfluous water
And nobody knew she was there.

CHORUS

The sixth to go in was old Mrs Murray
Who had to go in a bit of a hurry
But when she got there it was too late to worry
And nobody knew she was there.

SEEK DOO

Noo this wee doo wis seek,
it had hurted its beak,
wi stabbin a dod o' hard breed.
When alang came a boy,
jist a dirty wee boy,
wi' snotters and beasts in his heid.
The wee boy said: "Jings,
Ah' love aw' things wi wings"
and gied the wee doo a big cuddle,
sorted its beak
jist gave it a tweak,
and saftened its breed in a puddle.
Noo the doo gulped the breed,
it wis hunger, no greed,
and he said to the boy: "Thanks a lot,
fur yer jist a wee pet an' Ah'll never forget",
an the truth is he never forgot.
So aw you folk take heed,
never slap wee boys that huv beasts in their heid,
fur ye might slap the boy
that wis good tae the doo
an' the next thing the doo'll get you.

The above, which a chum of mine used to recite
about forty years ago, doesn't seem to have an author,

though it must have. The words are all I can find out about it. The usual pint of lager as a copyright fee for the author or his or her heirs and assignees.

18
GLASGOW JEWISH HUMOUR

Black? The ace of spades isny in it.

An elderly Weegie walks into a confessional. The following conversation ensues:

Man: "I am 92 years old, have a wonderful wife of 70 years, lots of children, grandchildren, and great grandchildren. Yesterday, I picked up two teenage girls, hitchhiking. We went to a hotel, where I had sex with each of them three times."

Priest: "Are you sorry for your sins?"

Man: "What sins?"

Priest: "What kind of a Catholic are you?"

Man: "I'm Jewish."

Priest: "Why are you telling me all this?"

Man: "I'm telling everybody."

I know a guy who describes himself as a Scottish Jew. He complains that it's hard being both Scottish and Jewish.

The Scottish part of him always wants to get pished, but the Jewish part of him doesn't want to pay for the drinks. Or maybe it is the other way round. By the end of the night he can't remember.

An archaeologist from Glasgow was digging in the Negev Desert in Israel and came upon a casket containing a mummy, a rather rare occurrence in Israel, to say the least. After examining it, he called the curator of the museum in Jerusalem.

"I've just discovered a 3,000-year-old mummy of a man who died of heart failure!" the excited scientist exclaimed.

To which the curator replied, "Bring him in. We'll check it out."

A week later, the amazed curator called the archaeologist. "You were right about both the mummy's age and cause of death. How in the world did you know?"

"Easy peasy. There was a piece of papyrus in his hand that said, '10,000 shekels on Goliath'."

19

GOOD ENOUGH FOR ME AND SADIE MCPHEE

A chum of mine, Bill Thompson, has a play, titled as above, what he has wrote. He can't get anyone to put it on, but it has some really funny songs in it, all about Weegie punters. Try these on for size.

TWO LITTLE BOYS

Words: Sean Tierney

Two little boys had two little toys
A whistle and a helmet too,
When they were wee, it was plain to see
What they'd grow up to do.
Hittin' aw the other weans, punchin' oot their
  brains,
Shoppin' everybody too.
They could never reform, now they're in uniform,
They're two little boys in blue.

CHORUS

Do you think I would leave you lying when I could
    lie my heid off too,
When some cunt squawks in the witness box
I'll cover up for you.
I'll tell a pack of lies, pull the wool over their eyes,
    the way the sergeant taught us to.
And when you count to three we'll all be off scot-
    free.
We're two little boys in blue.

Now the duty sergeant said tuck the prisoners up
    in bed but before you take their cocoa through,
Get them in the cells, hit them where it tells but
    don't leave them black and blue.
Knee them in the Kelvin haws, bash their heids
    against the wa's, get them in the kidneys too,
Belt their knees and thighs, but don't gie them
    black eyes,
Or we'll all be prisoners too.

CHORUS

If you see them in the street, pounding down the
    beat,
Here's my advice for you.
Don't trust to luck, turn around and run like fuck.
From the two little boys in blue.

THE MULLGUY SONG

Tune: Jumbalaya
Words: Sean Tierney

Goodbye Glasgow we're gonny go away oot bye-o.
Oot tae the West and get the best that money can
buy-o,
This Shangri-la is no' too far fae the toon-o
Jist faur enough tae keep yous scruff fae comin
roon-o.

CHORUS
In Mullguy the folks would die if they knew-o
Aw the times I had to sign down on the broo-o
These days are past I've lived life fast I can't deny-o
I've knocked it off I'm a hauf-biled toff fae
Mullguy-o.
This ideal home has a concrete gnome in the
garden,
It's the nearest thing that there is tae a hard-man.
Nae bugs or fleas, dugs daein pees in your back-
close-o
For everything in Mullguy is so so-so.
Me and the wife we've had a good life, *la Dolce
Vita*
Though at times we used tae pauchle the gas-
meter

Now playing whist, discreetly pissed on the fly-o
Ye never know what you've missed in Mullguy-o.

CHORUS

Sex is in, it's great tae swing with the fast-set-o
In this X-rated, sex-fixated suburban ghetto
To the beetle-drives that ruled our lives we've said
   goodbye-o
Ye get better vibes swapping wives in Mullguy-o.

CHORUS

DRIVELLIN' DOLL

Tune: Living Doll
Words: Sean Tierney

Got myself a drunken, boozing, false-teeth losing
   Drivellin' Doll.
Got to drink as much as she can, just cos she's my
   Drivellin' Doll.
Bevvies every night, she looks a fright, she's into
   alcohol
Got my one and only sprawlin', brawlin' Drivellin'
   Doll.

Take a sniff at her breath, its hell, if you don't
   believe what I say just smell.
Gonna wrap her up in a trunk so no big drunk can
   steal her away from me.
Got myself a steamin', stinking, vodka-drinking,
   dribbling doll.
Got myself a never-endin', elbow-bendin', dribbling
   doll,
She is never dry and that is why she drives me up
   the wall,
Got myself a stewin', spewing, fou yin Drivellin
   Doll.

GOOD ENOUGH FOR ME AND SADIE MCPHEE

Tune: Me and Bobby Magee
Words: Sean Tierney

Busted flat at Brigton Cross, shoutin' at the weans,
We'd just been barred oot the New Orleans,
Sadie thumbed a taxi doon, just before the rain,
Took us aw the way tae Jeannie Deans,
I ripped the ring-pull off a can a super lager,
Sooked away while Sadie took off her shoes,
Wae Sadie's bare feet slappin' time,
We gave it that ol' Mammy mine,
We gave the poor old driver dog's abuse.

CHORUS
 Being pissed was easy then when Sadie sank the
    booze
And Govan was a nice wee place tae be,
Being skint was just another word for havin' nae
    mair booze,
And the Buckie was good enough for me,
Good enough for me and Sadie McPhee.

From the closes of Camlachie tae the streets of
    Polmadie,
Sadie shared the secrets of my soul,
Through aw the time I done, Lord,
She just kept signing on the dole,
One day near the Barras, Lord, I let her slip away,
    she was looking for a close to have a pee,
I'd trade all my tomorrows for a drink of the
    Lannie wine, to be holdin' Sadie's bottle close to
    mine.

CHORUS

20

WISDOM, WHICH, AS YOU KNOW, CAN BE VERY, VERY DAFT INDEED

Eternity is very, very long, especially towards the end.

Some advice:
Do not ever answer the question: "Think yer a ticket?" Tickets get ripped (and/or) punched. Walk rapidly away from the questioner whistling 'The Sash'. You are probably going to get a doing anyway and there's around a fifty percent chance he'll be a Hun.

If he is wearing a green and white scarf, or any shade of green for that matter, whistle 'Sean South of Garryowen'. If it is a woman asking the question, run.

Our ice cream man was found lying on the floor of his van covered with hundreds and thousands. Police say that he topped himself.

When Jock Stein was asked if Kenny's best position was in midfield or attack, he said, "Och, just let him on the park," which is both wise and witty.

"They don't realise that there is no word in Glasgow for 'happy'. The nearest we have is 'giro' or 'blootered'."

Rab C.

"I'm rich and I'm Scottish. It doesn't get any better than that."

Craig Ferguson in a strange movie called I'll Be There *in which he played an aging rock star and the father of Charlotte Church.*

Pals are people who help you be more yourself.

Your body is a temple, but keep the spirits on the outside.

These days my body is more of a bouncy castle than a temple.

What discovery have you made if you find bones on the moon?

The cow didn't make it.

A friend of mine texted me yesterday to tell me he had been taken into hospital. I called him back straight away, as I was worried. He said the reason he was in was because he'd eaten what he thought was an onion, but turned out to be a daffodil bulb. The doctor says he'll be out in spring.

Here is a blessing: "May the best day of your past be the worst day of your future."

What do you get if you cross the Atlantic on the *Titanic*?
   About halfway.

I laugh in the face of danger. And then I hide until it goes away.

Modesty is the gentle art of enhancing one's charm by pretending not to be aware of it.

There have been many definitions of hell, but for the Scots the best definition is that it is the place where the Germans cook the food, the Swedish are the comedians, the Italians are the defence force, Frenchmen dig the roads, the Belgians are the pop singers, the Spanish run the railways, the English are the police and are brilliant at football, the Irish are the waiters, the Greeks run the government, and the common language is Dutch.

One day, a man came home and was greeted by his wife dressed in a very sexy nightie. "Tie me up," she purred, "and you can do anything you want."

So he tied her up and went to the golf club.

A Pollokshields woman came home, screeched her car into the drive and ran into the house. She slammed the door and shouted at the top of her lungs, "Harry, pack your bags. I've won the lottery!"

The husband said, "Jesus! Brilliant! What should I pack? Beach stuff, city stuff, hill stuff?"

"Doesn't matter," she said. "Just fuck off."

In Glasgow, marriage is a relationship in which one person is always right.

And the other is a husband.

You don't have to be a beer drinker to play darts, but it helps.

"I work until pub o'clock."

Glasgow freelance writer. Okay, me.

Advice to a youngster about his first job: "Work hard and keep your mouth S-H-U-T. Oh, except at dinnertime."

No man is an island, except in his bath.
Hugh MacDonald, Herald writer.

Quote from an early episode of *River City*, Glasgow's verra ain soap, about an accident victim who had been brain-damaged and who subsequently died: "Better deid than daft, eh."

These four folk were walking down the street – a Saudi, a Russian, a North Korean, and a Glaswegian. A reporter comes running up and says, "Excuse me, what is your opinion about the meat shortage?"

The Saudi says, "What's a shortage?"

The Russian says, "What's meat?"

The North Korean says, "What's an opinion?"

The Glaswegian says, "Excuse me? What's excuse me?"

Sometimes the road less travelled is less travelled for a reason.

If you want rainbows – you have to put up with the rain.

It's nice to be nice.

A Weegie Prayer
Grant me the serenity to accept the things I cannot change, the courage to change the things I cannot accept. And the wisdom to hide the bodies of the people I had to kill today because they pissed me off.

If the biscuit tin is always full, where's the fun in biscuits?

A healthy attitude is contagious, but don't wait to catch it from others. Be a carrier.

Criteria for a Glasgow mental home
"Well," said the director, "we fill up a bath, then we offer a teaspoon, a teacup, and a bucket to the patient and ask him or her to empty it."

"Oh, I understand," said the Edinbugger visitor. "A normal person would use the bucket because it's bigger than the spoon or the teacup."

"Actually," said the director, "a normal person would just pull the plug. So tell me, do you want a room with an east view or a west view?"

Police are called to a house in Bearsden and find a woman holding a bloody 5-iron standing over a lifeless man. The polis asks, "Is that your husband, Madam?"

"Yes," says the woman.

"Did you hit him with that golf club?"

"Yes, yes, I did." The woman begins to sob, drops the club, and puts her hands on her face.

"How many times did you hit him?"

"I don't know – five, six, maybe seven times – just put me down for a five."

A successful farmer died and left everything to his devoted wife. She was a very good-looking woman and determined to keep the farm, but knew very little about farming, so she decided to place an ad in the newspaper for an orra man.

Two men applied for the job. One was gay and the other a drunk. She thought long and hard about it, and when no one else applied she decided to hire the gay guy, figuring it would be safer to have him around the house than the drunk.

He proved to be a hard worker who put in long hours every day and knew a lot about farming. For weeks the two of them worked, and the farm was doing very well. Then one day, the widow said to the man, "You have done a really good job, and the cattle look great. You should go to the pub and have a laugh." The guy readily agreed and went into town on Saturday night.

One o'clock came, however, and he didn't return. Two o'clock, and no sign of him. He returned around two thirty, and upon entering the room, he found the widow sitting by the fireplace with a glass of wine, waiting for him. She quietly called him over to her.

"Unbutton my blouse and take it off," she said. Trembling, he did as she directed. "Now take off my boots." He did as she asked, very slowly. "Now take off my socks."

He removed each gently and placed them neatly by her boots. "Now take off my skirt." He slowly unbuttoned it, constantly watching her eyes in the firelight. "Now take off my bra." Again, with trembling hands, he did as he was told and dropped it to the floor. "Now," she said, "take off my panties."

By the light of the fire, he slowly pulled them down and off.

Then she looked at him and said, "If you ever wear my clothes again, you're fired."

A man goes into a sex shop and asks for a full size inflatable doll. The assistant asked if he wanted a man or woman and he chose a female. The assistant then asked if he wanted a white one or a black one.

He said that a black one would be fine.

Finally he was asked if he wanted a Christian or a Muslim. The man asked what religion had to do with buying a doll.

The assistant said: "The Muslim doll blows itself up."

"The nerve endings," said Gabriel. "How many will I put in her hands?"

"How many did we put in Adam?" asked the Lord, whom everyone knows is a Weegie.

"Two hundred, O Mighty One," replied Gabriel.

"Then we shall do the same for this woman," said The Lord.

"How many nerve endings should we put in the woman's genitals?" inquired Gabriel.

"How many did we put in Adam?" asked the Lord.

"Four hundred and twenty, O Mighty One," replied Gabriel.

"Of course. We did want Adam to have a means of receiving extra pleasure in his life, didn't we? Do the same for the woman," said the Lord.

"Yes, O Great Lord," said Gabriel.

"No, wait!" said the Lord. "Sod it, give the women ten thousand. I want them screaming out my name."

A wee Glesga man and a woman who have never met before find themselves in the same sleeping carriage of a train. After the initial embarrassment, they both manage to get to sleep, the woman on the top bunk, the man on the lower.

In the middle of the night, the woman leans over and says: "I'm sorry to bother you, but I'm freezing and I was wondering if you could possibly pass me another blanket."

The man leans out and with a glint in his eye, says, "I've got a better idea. Let's kid on wir married."

"Why not," giggles the woman.

"Good," he replies. "Get your own blanket."

Why don't you ever iron a four-leaf clover?

You don't want to press your luck.

Bob had finally made it to the last round of the big money quiz. The night before the big question, he told the host that he wanted a question on Scottish history.

The big night had arrived. Bob made his way on stage in front of the studio and TV audience. He had become the talk of the week and was the best guest this show had ever seen. The host stepped up to the mike.

"Bob, you have chosen Scottish history as your

final question. You know that if you correctly answer this question, you will walk away one million pounds richer. Are you ready?"

Bob nodded with a cocky confidence. He hadn't missed a question all week. "Bob, your question on Scottish history is a two-part question. As you know, you may answer either part first. As a rule, the second half of the question is easier. Which part would you like to take a stab at first?"

Bob was now becoming more noticeably nervous. He couldn't believe it, but he was drawing a blank. Scottish history was his best subject, but he played it safe. "I'll try the easier part first."

The host nodded approvingly. "Here we go Bob. I will ask you the second half first, then the first half."

The audience was silent in anticipation.

"Bob, here is your question:

"And in what year did it happen?"

Overheard in an East End pub, as a somewhat over-refreshed youth attempted to start singing a sectarian song. The tough-looking guy beside him at the bar closed his hand over the young man's mouth and said: "Be drunk or be stupid, son. Don't be both."

21
THE LAST CHAPTER:
A TRUE STORY, A WARNING, A SONG,
A PLEA AND A COMPLETE LIE

A woman called Senga meets a man called Shug in a pub in Govan. They talk, they connect, they end up leaving together. They get back to his place, and as he shows her around his flat, she notices that one wall of his bedroom is completely filled with soft, sweet, cuddly teddy bears. There are three shelves in the bedroom, with hundreds and hundreds of cute, cuddly teddy bears, carefully placed in rows covering the entire wall.

It was obvious that he had taken quite some time to lovingly arrange them and she was immediately touched by the amount of thought he had put into organizing the display. There were small bears along the bottom shelf, medium-sized bears covering the length of the middle shelf and huge, enormous bears running all the way along the top shelf. She found it strange for an obviously masculine guy to have such a large collection of teddy bears, but doesn't mention this to him, and actually is quite impressed by his sensitive side.

They share a bottle of wine, continue talking and, after a wee while, she finds herself thinking: "Oh my God! Maybe, this guy could be the one. Maybe he could be the future father of my children?"

She turns to him and kisses him lightly on the lips. He responds warmly. They continue to kiss, the passion builds, and he romantically lifts her in his arms and carries her into his bedroom where they rip off each other's clothes and make hot, steamy love. She is so overwhelmed that she responds with more passion, more creativity, more heat than she has ever known.

After an intense, explosive night of raw passion with this sensitive guy, they are lying there together in the afterglow. Senga rolls over, gently strokes his chest and asks coyly, "Well, how was it?"

Shug gently smiles at her, strokes her cheek, looks deeply into her eyes, and says, "Help yourself to any bear from the bottom shelf."

Those nice monks have accepted the Health Board's suggestion that the following warning labels be placed immediately on all varieties of Buckfast bottles.

WARNING

The consumption of Buckfast may leave you wondering what happened to your bra and knickers.

The consumption of Buckfast may make you think you are whispering when you are not.

The consumption of Buckfast is a major factor in dancing like a complete eejit.

The consumption of Buckfast may cause you to tell your friends over and over again that you love them.

The consumption of Buckfast may cause you to think you can sing, and should be avoided if the only song you know is 'I Will Survive', especially if you are a bloke.

The consumption of Buckfast may lead you to believe that ex-lovers are really dying for you to telephone them at four in the morning.

The consumption of Buckfast may make you think you can logically converse with members of the opposite sex without spitting.

The consumption of Buckfast may create the illusion that you are cleverer, faster and better looking than most people, and that you can fight.

The consumption of Buckfast may lead you to think people are laughing WITH you.

*

A dram can only apply to a measure of Scotch whisky, the size of which is determined by the generosity of the pourer, so in Glasgow and the West it is a dram, in Aberdeen and the North East the slightly smaller-sounding drammie, and in certain circles in Edinburgh and the East Coast, a dramlet, a very tiny thing indeed, which is also a little-known Shakespeare play about whisky, a Danish prince, and what a miserable bunch of bastards the Edinbuggers are.

"I'm sorry, sir," said the young barman with a discreet but meaningful glance at my waistline, "but I couldn't serve you another pie. I'd be breaking the law. And don't even think about chips." Pause. Another glance. "Or a roll."

This chilling scenario for us pie, chip and roll fans could be playing itself out in a pub near you in the near future if the Scottish Executive's new discussion document, which sets out a series of very iffy conditions for new publicans, ever makes it to the statute books.

They are currently considering whether or not to make it law that landlords must provide "sensible eating" advice to their punters so that they can continue to serve them booze, which we all know they never knowingly serve too much of to anyone, including that guy hanging on to your arm, saying, "You're my best pal, you are. I love you, mate."

Here is a confession. I am the (inordinately proud) owner of a Golden Pie Award, which was presented to me by David MacLennan at Oran Mor in Glasgow, which hosts the A Play, A Pie and A Pint series of lunchtime plays, of which David is the promoter. My Golden Pie was titled the Get a Life Award, as I have been to every single one of the plays, at the time of writing seventy-eight, which means that I have eaten (and enjoyed, the Oran Mor pies are terrific) the same number of round meaty pastry things, not to mention the pints, of which there were a number that I would like to remain uncounted.

I do not wish to attend a series of works titled A

Play, We'll Measure You Up For a Pie and We'll Give You a Blood Test Before We Even Consider Serving You a Pint. I do not want to hear people saying: "Beans? But you broke wind in here last week, madam. The emissions were measured and I'm afraid you don't qualify for beans in the foreseeable future". And I do not wish to be told what to do by Union Jack McConnell and his increasingly petty and meddling minions.

The smoking ban I agree with. It was harming people who did not wish to smoke, including me, and from a selfish point of view, it has increased my enjoyment and expectation of life, is saving me money and helping the environment. To explain, I enjoy my food and drink in the pub a lot more than I did, I've decreased my risk of cancer and I don't have to wash my clothes nearly as much, so I'm not polluting the water system as often.

But this latest plan is the thin end of a very thick wedge indeed. Tony Blair might be leading us more or less unprotestingly down his deluded path to the kind of crypto-fascist state in which the Scottish Executive's suggestions/laws might be seen as reasonable, but here in Scotland we have surely got more sense than that. If this sort of thinking is allowed to continue it could be: "Going to the football? Not with your heart condition, laddie."

Basic rights are being infringed here. If I, as is the God-given right of every Glaswegian, wish to cover the entire front of my clothing in rancid grease of a Friday evening as I consume a Grecian delicacy, or wake up with my face in a poke of over-vinegared chips (don't ask), I should be allowed to do so. Who am I harming, apart from myself? I do not wish anyone to tell me what I should or should not eat, and I especially do not wish to hand over my right to eat whatever I damn well choose to the kind of people who have happy hours and sell alcohol, a very powerful drug, to people who can't handle it.

Here's my plan. If this stupidity becomes law, I will open a place called Carbohydrates R Us, a kind of shebean, if you like, where you can illicitly slabber beans over your greasy bridie or batter butter into your mash without fear of nanny-state control freaks telling you what is good for you.

Eat pies now! Drink tons! Fat is freedom!

More advice
Never play leapfrog with a unicorn.

Do not meddle in the affairs of dragons, for you are crunchy, and taste very good with brown sauce.

Do not enter a battle of wits unarmed.

One more wee song I've just remembered:

> Oh, dear me, my Granny caught a flea
> She salted it and peppered it
> And hud it fur her tea.
> My Granny didny like it
> She gave it to her son
> Her son didny like it
> He threw it up the lum.
> The lum gave a crack
> The hoose gave a shak
> And doon came Granny wi' her shirt a' black.

And finally.

It's not that I drink too much or that I particularly want to live for ever, it's just that I'm going to have to stick around until the Atomic Energy Authority finds a safe place to bury my liver.